BEGINNER CURSIVE HANDWRITING WORKBOOK FOR KIDS

Learn and Practice Cursive with Confidence

Crystal Radke

Illustrations by Amir Abou Roumie

ROCKRIDGE PRESS

For general information on our other products and services or to obtain technical support, please contact our Customer Care Department within the United States at (866) 744-2665, or outside the United States at (510) 253-0500.

Rockridge Press publishes its books in a variety of electronic and print formats. Some content that appears in print may not be available in electronic books, and vice versa.

Interior and Cover Designer: Jami Spittler
Art Producer: Megan Baggott
Editor: Jeanann Pannasch
Production Editor: Matthew Burnett
Production Manager: Riley Hoffman

Illustrations © 2021 Amir Abou Roumie. Author photograph courtesy of Twenty Toes Photography LLC.

Paperback ISBN: 978-1-63878-148-6
R0

The *Write* Start

Welcome to this workbook! Did you know that we use a different part of our brain when we write in cursive compared to when we print or type? By writing in cursive, you are improving important thinking skills and language skills and working your memory.

As you progress through the book, make sure to read through the instructions in each section. Make sure you go in order, too. The exercises are specially organized to help you be successful. You might find it helpful to tilt the book as you write; angle it a little to the right if you are right handed and left if you are left handed.

You will start by learning how to form each letter of the alphabet. In each affirmation, we've included a demonstration of the practice letter in that sentence—in uppercase or lowercase—to reflect the example on each page. Then you will *learn* how to connect some common two- and three-letter combinations. Finally, you'll form words and write full sentences.

This cursive writing book will teach you more than just how to write in cursive. It will also help remind you how awesome you are. The affirmations aren't just to practice writing; they are all statements about *you*! When you read the emphasized words that go along with each letter, proudly believe that they are true for your life.

You'll be stimulating your brain, feeling empowered, and learning how to write in cursive. Wow! You are going to love this book.

Happy writing.

Trace and write the cursive letter.

Trace and write the cursive letter.

Every day offers a
new *Adventure.*

Trace and write the cursive letter.

When I try
new things,
I am *brave*.

6

Always *Bee-lieve* in yourself.

Trace and write the cursive letter.

Trace and write the cursive letter.

Today is a
new *chance.*

If it doesn't *Challenge* me, it won't *Change* me.

Trace and write the cursive letter.

d

Trace and write the cursive letter.

Trace and write the cursive letter.

Don't be afraid
to *Dream* big.

Trace and write the cursive letter.

Trace and write the cursive letter.

I am *Enough.*

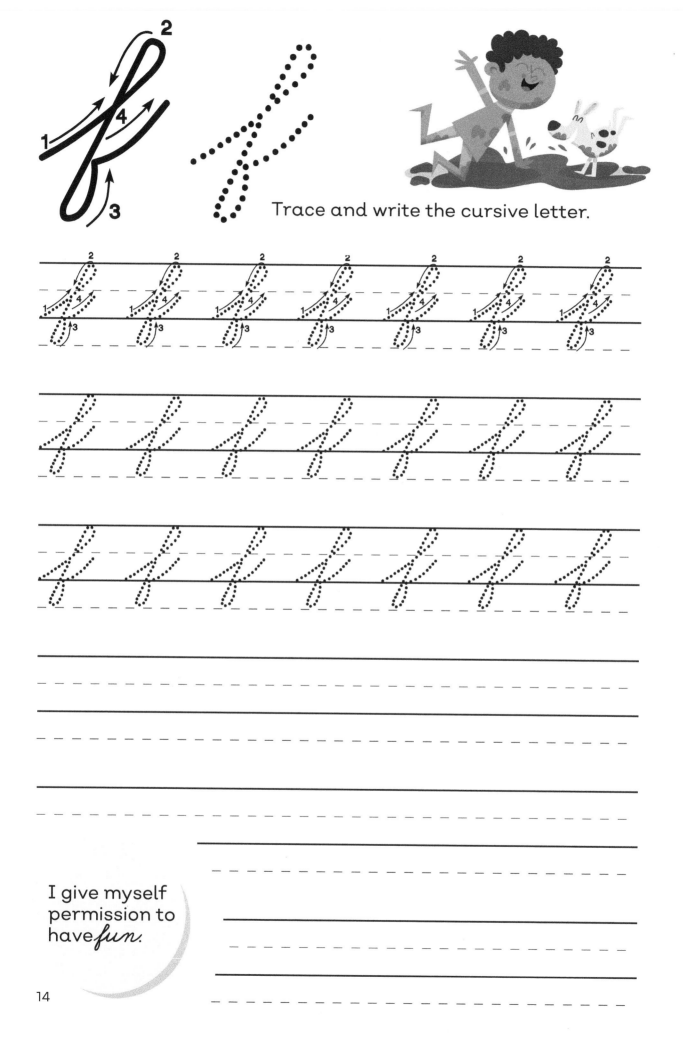

Trace and write the cursive letter.

I give myself permission to have *fun.*

I can be a
Fantastic Friend.

Trace and write the cursive letter.

Trace and write the cursive letter.

I choose to focus on the *good*.

Trace and write the cursive letter.

Mistakes help me *Grow.*

17

Trace and write the cursive letter.

Trace and write the cursive letter.

Hard things aren't impossible; they just take longer to figure out.

Trace and write the cursive letter.

Trace and write the cursive letter.

I can *Inspire* others with my words and actions.

Trace and write the cursive letter.

I stand for
justice for
everyone.

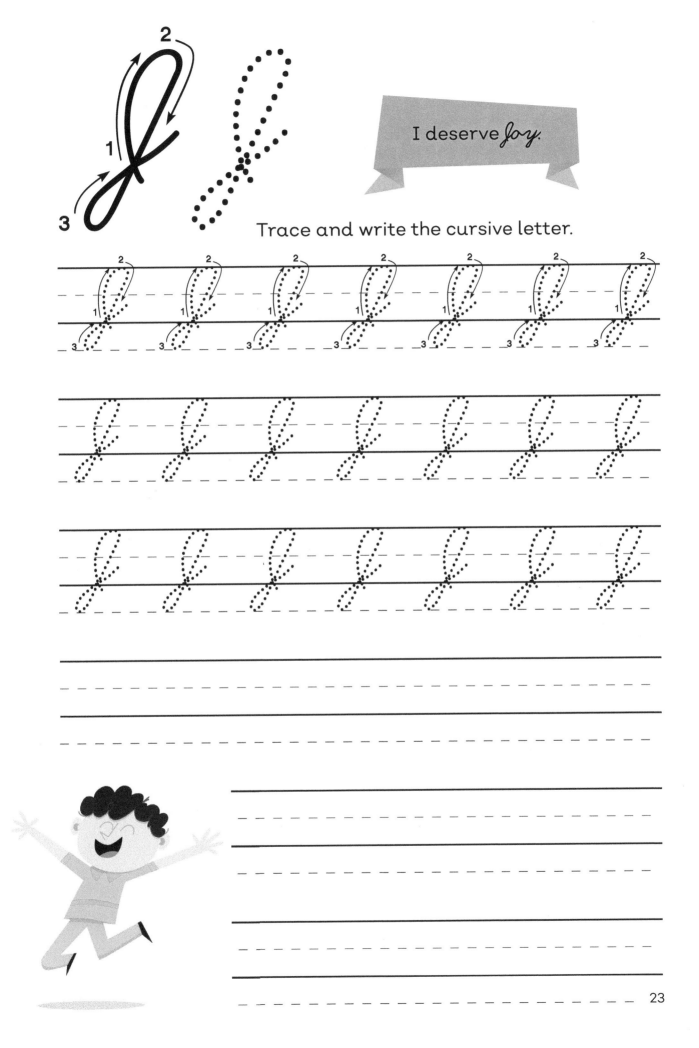

I deserve *Joy*.

Trace and write the cursive letter.

Trace and write the cursive letter.

If you never try, you'll never *know*.

I plant *Kindness*
wherever I go.

Trace and write the cursive letter.

25

Trace and write the cursive letter.

Just by being me, I *light* up a room.

Trace and write the cursive letter.

The best *Luck* is the
Luck you make yourself.

Trace and write the cursive letter.

Trace and write the cursive letter.

I believe in *Myself.*

$\mathcal{M}$ m

Trace and write the cursive letter.

I *never* give up!

We *need* each other.

Trace and write the cursive letter.

Trace and write the cursive letter.

There is *only one* you.

My mind learns
when it is *Open.*

Trace and write the cursive letter.

Trace and write the cursive letter.

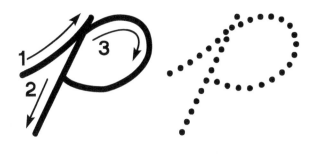

Trace and write the cursive letter.

Difficult roads lead to sweet Places.

With friends, I choose *quality* over *quantity*.

Trace and write the cursive letter.

36

Trace and write the cursive letter.

Even when I'm *Quiet,* my words have power.

Trace and write the cursive letter.

You can't have a *rainbow* without a little *rain.*

Trace and write the cursive letter.

When the earth needs extra care, I am *Ready*.

Trace and write the cursive letter.

I am *stronger* than peer pressure.

Trace and write the cursive letter.

Trace and write the cursive letter.

42

Trace and write the cursive letter.

I don't survive, I *Thrive*.

Trace and write the cursive letter.

Trace and write the cursive letter.

I am *Unstoppable*
and will never give *Up.*

Trace and write the cursive letter.

I can
visualize
my
achievements.

Trace and write the cursive letter.

My opinions are *Valuable*.

47

Trace and write the cursive letter.

Every now
and then, it's fun
to *walk* on
the *wild*
side.

Trace and write the cursive letter.

Trace and write the cursive letter.

Trace and write the cursive letter.

Trace and write the cursive letter.

52

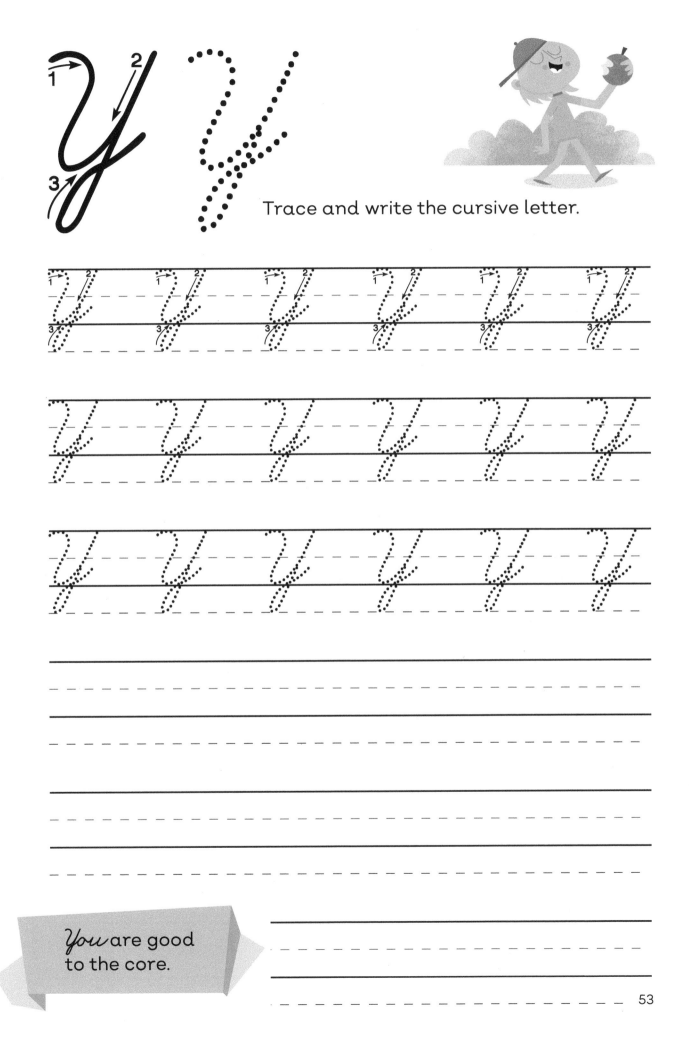

Trace and write the cursive letter.

You are good
to the core.

Trace and write the cursive letter.

I have a *zest* for life.

I can *zoom* in on love.

Trace and write the cursive letter.

ai *ai*

Br *Br*

ch *ch*

Du *Du*

el *el*

Fl *Fl*

Trace and write connecting cursive letters.

Trace and write connecting cursive letters.

mp   mp

na   na

oe   oe

Pu   Pu

qu   qu

Ri   Ri

Trace and write connecting cursive letters.

Sc Sc

Tr Tr

ue ue

Va Va

wo wo

Xe Xe

Trace and write connecting cursive letters.

Awareness

Brilliant

Caring

devoted

Excited

funny

Grateful

happy

Inspiring

joyful

Knowledgable

lovely

Motivating

nice

Outgoing

positive

Quick

island

Smart

thoughtful

Useful

vibrant

Wonderful

animal

Yourself

gist

My dreams can

come true.

Today is a

fresh start.

I can learn

new things.

I am worthy of love.

I am a role
model.

Every swimmer

was once a

beginner.

The time is now

to be who I

want to be.

I do not have

to be perfect to

be amazing.

Start each day

with a grateful

heart.

I am awesome

because

CRYSTAL RADKE is an educational leader, speaker, and bestselling author. After spending time as a kindergarten teacher, she began her consulting business where she mentors educators, providing inspirational keynotes and powerful professional development. Her two degrees in early childhood education and her experience as a foster and adoptive mother have made helping children learn and grow a personal mission.